DAILY GUIDEPOSTS

....

40 DEVOTIONS FOR LENT

EDITORS OF GUIDEPOSTS

New York

ZONDERVAN®

ZONDERVAN

Daily Guideposts: 40 Devotions for Lent
Copyright © 2017 by Guideposts

Requests for information should be addressed to:
Zondervan, *3900 Sparks Dr. SE, Grand Rapids, Michigan 49546*

ISBN 978-0-310-35022-4 (softcover)

ISBN 978-0-310-35083-5 (ebook)

Bible translations quoted in this book are listed on pages 87–88,
which hereby become a part of this copyright page.

Cover design: Müllerhaus
Cover photo: Shutterstock®
Interior design: Kait Lamphere

First printing November 2016 / Printed in the United States of America

Hello, friend.

Through the dark days of winter, it's hard to remember that spring is coming. Night falls early, chills seem endless, and we long for just one flower to poke out of the cold ground. But even in winter, the days begin to grow longer, and we slowly move toward the next season when everything comes to life again. The rhythm of the natural world is a beautiful reminder of the hope of Christ—that the problems of this world are only one season of life.

In John 11, we read the story of two sisters, Mary and Martha, who were mourning the death of their brother, Lazarus. They were all friends of Jesus. Although the sisters had sent word to Him when Lazarus became sick, Jesus didn't arrive until four days after their brother died. The air must have been heavy with grief. "Lord . . . if you had been here, my brother would not have died," Martha says (John 11:21, NIV). Jesus tells Martha that death doesn't mark the end. He speaks in mystery: "I am the resurrection and the life"

(John 11:25, NIV). Then He calls Lazarus out of the tomb.

And what joy that the story doesn't end there! Jesus Himself rose from the dead. Jesus's winter season of being captured, beaten, and killed, dying on the Cross, gave way to hope eternal, the power over death resulting in everlasting life for all who believe. Jesus says in John 16:33 (NIV), "In this world you will have trouble. But take heart! I have overcome the world."

For the next six weeks and culminating with a special devotion for Easter Sunday, join us in reflecting on Jesus the Christ—His life, death, burial, and Resurrection. Our hope is that you will be drawn nearer to God and be encouraged to hold on to hope, never losing sight of the spring that is coming.

Blessings,
Editors of Guideposts

THE FIRST DAY: *ASH WEDNESDAY*

THE MARK OF THE HEALER

With his stripes we are healed. —Isaiah 53:5 *(KJV)*

"Good morning, Erin," I said first thing that February day. She was working at the reception desk and I was rushing to my office. "How are you?" I asked rather automatically. I had a thousand things on my mind.

"Fine," she replied. Something in her voice made me stop.

"What's wrong?"

"I was in a car accident last night." Her lip quivered, and I noticed the bump on her forehead.

"Are you all right?"

"I thought I was. I wasn't hurt much. I'm lucky. The other driver ran a red light. But now I'm feeling kind of shaky."

"If you need to go home . . ."

"No. I'd rather be here. I need to be around people." Others arrived, and we listened to her, somebody got her some coffee, and the volunteer

EMT in the office inspected her forehead more closely. Reassured that Erin would be okay, we went to our desks, but we were all left wondering what more we could do. An ice pack? Aspirin? Could I get her some lunch?

At midday she was gone. "She went out," someone told me. *Good*, I thought. *She'll get some fresh air, some lunch.* When I returned from my lunch, she was back at the front desk and looked a lot more relaxed.

"I'm feeling much better," she said.

But your forehead, I was about to say. There was a dark smudge over the bump. Had the bruise gotten worse? Then I remembered the day: Ash Wednesday, when some of our fellow believers in Christ observe the start of Lent with a bit of ash in the shape of a cross. Erin's smudge was the mark of the Healer.

"You found the right place to go at lunch," I said.

"It helped a lot," she added.

In faith, Lord, I turn to You for healing. —Rick Hamlin

Digging Deeper: *Isaiah 41:10; Matthew 14:13–14; 1 Peter 2:24*

THE SECOND DAY: *THURSDAY*

RED WORDS

If a man love me, he will keep my words:
and my Father will love him. —John 14:23 (KJV)

Words. I am surrounded by them. As an editor, I poke and scratch and rework them. As a writer, I try to make them sing. As an avid magazine and newspaper reader, I use them to gather information. But sometimes I think there are too many words in the world—or at least, in my world.

So for Lent this year, I'm reading only certain words in my Bible. The words of Jesus. They are conveniently printed in red—bright patches of scarlet among all the lines of black. When I leaf through the Gospels, I see that Jesus is, indeed, a man of few words. "Let your light shine" (Matthew 5:16). "Love your enemies" (Matthew 5:44). "Come and follow me" (Matthew 19:21). "Make disciples of all nations" (Matthew 28:19). "I am the resurrection and the life" (John 11:25).

I find comfort in His words. But I find challenge too. There is an energy in their sparseness. It makes much of my world seem unduly wordy. It makes much of what I say seem unduly wordy. I begin to understand: More is not always better.

So during this holy season, I will immerse myself in the red words. They are my salvation.

Dear Jesus, let me find quiet time to meditate on the most important words ever spoken: Yours. —Mary Lou Carney

Digging Deeper: *John 1:1, 14:15; Hebrews 4:12*

....

THE THIRD DAY: *FRIDAY*

MARY'S GIFT

And whosoever shall exalt himself shall be abased; and he that shall humble himself shall be exalted. —Matthew 23:12 (KJV)

My son is withdrawn, dull-eyed. My husband thinks John is depressed, and I agree. It's time to get help. This is a hard step for us: We like to think of ourselves as competent and capable, not as failures who can't guide a six-year-old through his troubles. But we have held on to our pride too long already.

I bring John in for a full medical and psychiatric exam. Turning my son over for professionals to evaluate is rough. I do not want to cede what little control I have.

It strikes me that this feeling is not new. All too often when I finally, fully turn something over to God, it has my claw marks on it. I hold on, I waffle, I give some but not all. Today I hunt through Scripture for a better understanding of what it means to give to Christ completely. This time it's Mary with her alabaster jar of nard who gives me insight (Matthew 26:6–13).

Truthfully, I've never made a material sacrifice for God as generous as Mary's gift. I'm not sure if I even own anything that is worth an entire year's wages. Yet Mary gave her whole nest egg of nard to Christ without being asked.

Judas was partially right: It was an extravagant gift. What he didn't grasp was that the cost was not to be counted in silver but in love. Christ saw first and foremost the lavish outpouring of Mary's heart. She anointed the King of love with her love, in preparation for His entry into His kingdom.

I want to love my family that way. I want to love Christ as Mary did. But I know such extravagance can't exist when I insist on being the one who is in control of my life. To love Christ fully, I must first remove the stopper of pride from my heart.

Oh, teach me to love with extravagance, my Lord!
—Julia Attaway

Digging Deeper: *Jeremiah 10:23; Matthew 26:6–13; James 4:6*

....

THE FOURTH DAY: *SATURDAY*

RECEIVING THE BLESSING

The Lord bless thee, and keep thee: The Lord make his face shine upon thee, and be gracious unto thee: The Lord lift up his countenance upon thee, and give thee peace. —Numbers 6:24–26 (KJV)

In the closing moments of the Sunday morning service, our pastor raises his arms toward heaven and calls down the blessing of the Lord upon all of us in the congregation. I bow my head in the contemplative prayer that has become for me a pre-blessing ritual. I am a greedy child of God—I want every blessing, every gift the Lord has for me; I want nothing within me to hinder His giving or my receiving.

All too frequently, as I put down my hymnal and turn my hands palms-up to receive the blessing, I wince; I find my hands already full. Sometimes my fists are clenched, white knuckled, in unresolved anger, as they were the week a hit-and-run driver fatally injured our small calico cat. Sometimes I find myself holding on to brooding resentments over words spoken to me in the heat of an argument; or worse, I may be holding on to the guilt of harsh words I've spoken to others. Sometimes I'm clutching habitual worries I thought I'd let go the previous Sunday, only to find that through the days that followed I've picked them up again. So I begin my weekly ritual of letting go:

In these moments, Lord, I empty my hands and
    open them to You.
I let go of anger; fill and bless me with Your love.
I let go of guilt; fill and bless me with forgiveness.
I let go of self-pity; fill and bless me with a
    grateful heart.
I let go of worries and fear; fill and bless me
    with trust.
I let go of the hurts of the past; fill and bless me
    with the promise of the present.

Bless me and keep me, Lord. Let Your face shine upon me,
uphold me, and give me peace. —Fay Angus

Digging Deeper: *Psalm 84:11; Isaiah 40:31; James 1:17*

....

THE FIFTH DAY: *MONDAY*

BACK TO JERUSALEM

There is none good but one, that is, God.
    —Matthew 19:17 (KJV)

Jesus again leaves the village of Bethany for Jerusalem early in the morning. Eager listeners wait for Him in the temple. He has so much to teach in so little time.

Among the parables Jesus tells today is one about a marriage feast for a king's son. The king's invited guests didn't bother to come. So he called the poor and homeless from their hideouts and packed the wedding hall. They each donned a beautiful wedding garment provided by him, shed their poverty, and feasted with the king.

As Jesus tells the parable, I remember the homeless people I met in a park one morning when I was in South Dakota. One of them, Mike, had watery blue eyes, missing teeth, a grizzled red beard, and ears that stuck straight out. As we talked, I asked Mike if I could add him to the list of people I pray for each day. His eyes slid away from mine, and he barely whispered, "Yes."

I like to think that Mike, in his faded, mismatched secondhand garb, will end up clothed in wedding finery at the marriage feast in Jesus's parable. And as I listen to Jesus, I know that I am one the heavenly King has rescued too. Although I may look very different from Mike on the outside,

Jesus sees my interior poverty—my sins and my struggles. He knows that I'm in need of the garment of goodness only the King's Son can bestow.

Jesus—
Righteous Redeemer, revealed of God,
Holy the ground Thy feet have trod.
Thy steps upon my soul impress,
And there impart Thy holiness. —Carol Knapp

Digging Deeper: *Isaiah 61:10; Romans 3:10; 2 Corinthians 5:21*

....

THE SIXTH DAY: *TUESDAY*

FROM MANGER TO CROSS

Then Simeon blessed them and said to his mother Mary,
". . . and a sword will pierce your own soul too."
—Luke 2:34–35 (NRSV)

One of my Lenten lessons this year came right after Christmas. Our neighbor in New London,

Connecticut, assembled a glorious outdoor crèche with carved figures standing and kneeling on straw in a wooden stable. A strategically placed spotlight revealed the figures' expressions and positions. They are poor folk, from the weary parents to the ragged, adoring shepherds.

A few days after Christmas, we were hit by a nor'easter. The spotlight illuminated the crèche while the snow flew and the wind howled. When I looked outside, drifting snow had covered the figure of Baby Jesus. Goose bumps rose on my arms. There was something about the scene that disturbed me; I was seeing a preview of what was to come. The rejoicing of this birthday would lead to glory and grief.

Then I noticed that the figures around the manger appeared different, now that the baby was covered with snow. Their faces, especially Mary's and Joseph's, looked stunned and sorrowful. The angel no longer seemed to be radiantly singing praises but grimly keeping vigil. The shepherds' awe wasn't joyous astonishment but amazement that such a sacrifice would be made for them. Even the animals seemed to cower in grief.

Later that Christmas week, the sun came out

and melted the snow on the manger. And at the end of His painful journey, the Son Himself will rise and melt the ice around our grieving hearts.

Father, my heart cries out in joy at Your wondrous gift and in sorrow at Your wrenching sacrifice. —Marci Alborghetti

Digging Deeper: *Isaiah 53:5; Philippians 3:10–11*

....

THE SEVENTH DAY: *WEDNESDAY*

SMALL GIFTS

"Then shall the maidens rejoice in the dance, and the young men and the old shall be merry. I will turn their mourning into joy, I will comfort them, and give them gladness for sorrow." —Jeremiah 31:13 (RSV)

I was comparing notes about middle age with a friend. We brought up the usual complaints of men in their fifties: bad knees, complicated relationships, uncertain futures. "Sometimes I feel like I'm out at sea," I said.

"Which one are you?" my friend asked. "The *Titanic* or the iceberg?"

I laughed, but I'm not sure why. Which one am I, the engineering marvel full of doomed lives and hubris, or the shadowy iceberg lurking in the night, small on the surface but holding so much more underneath? Does destiny control me, or am I able to navigate what lies ahead?

Lent is a time for preparation, but it's also a time of renewal. There's some question about what Jesus did right before His last, fateful trip to Jerusalem; I'll go with the story in the Gospel of John—that Jesus was relaxed and renewed, anointed with oil. The oil was a small gift but the right gift. Jesus seemed to have a knack for foresight—surely He knew what was awaiting Him—but it was not the time to dwell on the week ahead.

For myself, I dunno. I hope I am neither the iceberg nor the ocean liner. Instead, I want to be known as the bass player in the *Titanic* dance band. Right now we're playing a nifty swing number and the crowd is merry as we toast our collective voyage. Soon enough we'll be playing "Nearer, My God, to Thee," but for now we relax, we dance. It's a small gift, but sometimes small gifts are all we have.

Lord, suffering awaits all flesh. Let me appreciate the small, joyful gifts of Your bounty as we prepare for what lies ahead. Amen. —Mark Collins

Digging Deeper: *Psalms 100, 106:1*

....

THE EIGHTH DAY: *THURSDAY*

A LENTEN MINISTRY

If any of you lacks wisdom, let him ask of God, who gives to all liberally and without reproach, and it will be given to him. —James 1:5 *(NKJV)*

Five years ago during Lent, I decided to write down my reflections about my daily devotional reading as a preparation for Easter. I e-mailed my daily reading/writing to my children and to friends who I thought would like them.

At first the project was awkward and almost

painful; I was trying too hard to write the perfect thing. Then I began to write whatever came from my heart. As the days turned into weeks, I found that I couldn't wait to get my morning chores done so I could escape to my computer corner. I could feel my faith growing with each passing day and I was surprised to find that my personal reflections actually taught me things about myself.

When Lent was over, I thought my project was finished and I stopped taking my daily time at the computer. Within days I received e-mails from my family and friends asking me what had happened to my daily e-mail.

Now my little Lenten project has grown into a real ministry. I print out my reflections for our morning guests here at the bed-and-breakfast, and many ask to be added to my ever-growing mailing list.

Lord, thank You for using me to touch the lives of others.
All that I do is for Your glory, day in and day out.
—Patricia Pusey

Digging Deeper: *Romans 12:6–8; 1 Corinthians 10:31*

THE NINTH DAY: *FRIDAY*

LETTING GO

For sin will have no dominion over you, since you are not under law but under grace. —Romans 6:14 *(NRSV)*

I've been told that swans mate for life. I don't know if that's true, but I do know they are very loyal parents. My husband, Charlie, and I have been watching two swans and their baby for a while, long enough to see the baby grow from a tiny creature carried on its parents' backs to a figure as impressive as its parents in everything but its gray plumage. Whenever we spot one swan, the other two aren't far away. The mother sticks very close to the youngster. If it veers off in a wayward direction, she's right behind. If it tries to befriend a group of ducks, she heads off any intermingling. The father is more nonchalant, gliding off in a show of majestic disdain but never too far. Lately, though, both parents are giving the baby more freedom. They stare after the young adventurer with what seems like longing and fear for its welfare, but they let it go anyway.

I understand that need to hold on. During Lent, I usually go to a reconciliation service, where I confess my sins and ask God's forgiveness. The problem is I find it hard to accept that forgiveness and to let go of my guilt. This year, my pastor looked me in the eye and said, "You do know, don't you, that this only works if you believe God has forgiven you and, therefore, you forgive yourself?"

I do *know* it; I don't always *feel* it. So now I'll try to imitate the swans and let go of what's no longer mine—what Jesus lived through to take from me.

Lord, give me the strength to lay the burden of my sins at the foot of Your Cross and to leave it there.
—Marci Alborghetti

Digging Deeper: *Isaiah 43:25–26; 2 Corinthians 5:17; 1 John 1:9*

THE TENTH DAY: *SATURDAY*

SCRUBBED CLEAN

Then will I sprinkle clean water upon you,
and ye shall be clean. —Ezekiel 36:25 *(KJV)*

My Maggie is an artist; she likes to draw. Being the exuberant soul she is, she prefers larger surfaces. A big white wall is irresistible; tabletops are attractive too. In a pinch Maggie will draw on herself if indelible markers are available.

Maggie's fascination with drawing is unique in my parenting experience. When she executed her first large-scale masterpiece, I used the technique that had worked with my other children: I handed her a sponge and made her scrub the wall. It was a big job for a two-and-a-half-year-old, and Maggie didn't like it at all. But the next day she rushed up to me eagerly and said, "I need a sponge, Mommy! I drawed on the floor!"

Such persistence is not a matter of mere stubbornness. For Maggie, the joy of swirling a crayon in full-arm rotation is so immense that it has nothing to do with the idea that she's only supposed to draw on paper. She doesn't realize she's being disobedient. Since she's only two, I don't find that particularly surprising. She has time to learn.

I'm a long way from being two. I no longer draw on walls, and I manage to avoid a lot of bigger no-no's. But there are still many times each day when I do what I feel like doing, without considering what God wants me to do. All too often it's only when I'm in bed mentally reviewing the day that I even realize that I was disobedient.

Unlike Maggie, I'm not always cheerful about saying I'm sorry. I'm never quite as willing to admit I've done wrong or as eager to get back to the drawing board. But maybe that will come with time.

I've done it again, Lord. Come, wash me clean.
—Julia Attaway

Digging Deeper: *Psalm 51:7; Isaiah 1:18; John 15:3*

THE ELEVENTH DAY: *MONDAY*

MORNING MERCIES

"For the mouth speaks what the heart is full of." —Luke 6:45 (NIV)

One morning before a church meeting, I said a quick prayer to keep me from saying negative or critical things. All went well until the end, when we discussed trying a new form of worship. Suddenly, a quick criticism fell right out of my mouth: "The powers that be won't like it, and they'll probably veto it." I immediately felt a twinge of guilt, but I pretended nothing was wrong.

After the meeting I knew it was time to visit the prayer chapel. As I knelt, I recalled that last Sunday in class we'd seen a video where the speaker had two glasses filled to the brim with beads. When he knocked them together, several beads popped out of both of them because of the impact. The speaker explained that we can't blame other people for bringing out the worst in us because nothing can come out of us that's not already in there to begin with. I left the chapel knowing I had been forgiven, but I still felt I'd let down God and myself.

Driving home, I hit road-construction traffic and turned off on a street I rarely take. As I was passing a church, my eye caught a message-board sign out front. "Jesus still loves you" was all it said. I let out a deep cleansing breath, thankful that not only are God's mercies new every morning but so is His unchanging love.

Dear Jesus, show me the hidden places inside of me where I need Your mercies every morning, so I can live better days for You. Amen. —Karen Barber

Digging Deeper: *Joel 2:12–13; Hebrews 4:16*

....

THE TWELFTH DAY: *TUESDAY*

FAITHFUL FRIENDS

I will sacrifice unto thee with the voice of thanksgiving. —Jonah 2:9 *(KJV)*

My childhood friend Lynda and I shared many happy times, especially with food. We cooked together, using the same child's cookbook; licked the beaters and bowl when her mom decorated yet another cake; and snuck downstairs to the fridge and cookie jar during sleepovers. Staying for a midday meal always meant a three-course feast.

During a lunch in late winter, I had finished my casserole when I was served a dreamy banana-pudding-and-whipped-cream parfait with a cherry on top, in a tall glass like a vase. I was enchanted, until I noticed that Lynda had been served a saucer of plain red gelatin, with no whipped cream. Lynda noticed my bewilderment.

"I gave up desserts for Lent," she said simply.

"What's that?"

"You get ready for Easter by giving up something you like."

Unbelievable! My nine-year-old brain simply couldn't grasp self-sacrifice of that magnitude. During the next few weeks I kept a closer eye on Lynda and her lunch box. Sure enough: no cupcakes, no cookies, no brownies. She had made a simple promise, and she kept it.

Inspired by Lynda, I gave up bubble gum the following Lent and candy the year after that. It took me until high school even to try giving up desserts.

I practice Lenten self-denial with a deeper understanding these days, all begun by the cheerful resolve of a little girl who gave up her pudding.

Lord, thank You for friends who draw us closer to You.
—Gail Thorell Schilling

Digging Deeper: *Ecclesiastes 4:9–12; Proverbs 27:17*

....

THE THIRTEENTH DAY: *WEDNESDAY*

LOVE ONE ANOTHER

"A new commandment I give to you, that you love one another, even as I have loved you, that you also love one another. By this all men will know that you are My disciples, if you have love for one another." —John 13:34–35 (NAS)

During His final trip to Jerusalem, Jesus knew that time was running out. He needed to tell His disciples the most important things to remember.

As He looked at the disciples who followed Him, their faces strained with anxiety and apprehension, Jesus was aware that love was being squeezed out of their hearts by fear. Anger and jealousy were surfacing; envy and competition were evident. In that moment Jesus turned to His followers and said, "A new commandment I give to you, that you love one another, even as I have loved you."

Jesus knew His disciples would be remembered by one thing: their ability to love everyone, even in the most difficult of times.

More than a thousand years later, a young man named Francis read the Gospels and gave his life to Christ. He began to love everyone, even animals, and to minister to them. He created a movement called the Lesser Brothers to bring love and compassion to the most desperate and poverty-stricken. In the rule that he made for them, he wrote, "Let all the brothers . . . preach by their deeds."

Jesus said it another way: "By this all men will know that you are My disciples, if you have love for one another."

Dear Father, may I use my actions this day to show others how much I love them. —Scott Walker

Digging Deeper: *Matthew 22:34–40*

....

THE FOURTEENTH DAY: *THURSDAY*

WATCHING OUR WORDS

Don't use bad language. Say only what is good and helpful to those you are talking to, and what will give them a blessing. —*Ephesians 4:29 (TLB)*

When I was writing radio commercials at a big Milwaukee radio station, one thing I didn't like about the job was the bad language around the office. Each day I watched the stress level of the sales staff increase as they struggled to make their projected sales. As tensions rose, the entire sales staff got into the habit of using foul language to let off steam.

One day, Tom, a radio salesman, mentioned a sermon he'd heard at church about the use of profanity. "You know," he said, "we really abuse it around here. Why don't we give up swearing for Lent? Each time one of us swears or curses, let's drop a quarter into a jar."

News of our Swear Jar quickly spread around the building of nearly three hundred employees, many of whom dropped in periodically to see how we were doing. Six weeks later a note appeared in our paycheck envelopes: "Congratulations to the AM Radio Sales Staff. Their Swear Jar full of 187 swears ($46.75) was delivered to the Rescue Mission this past Friday. AM Sales has decided to continue to watch their mouths and contribute to the jar when necessary."

Lord, if I'm ever tempted to let off steam with bad language, turn my words into a prayer instead. —Patricia Lorenz

Digging Deeper: *Psalm 19:14; Colossians 3:16; James 3:3–6*

The Fifteenth Day: *Friday*

Asking for Forgiveness

*Father, forgive them; for they know not
what they do. . . . —Luke 23:34 (KJV)*

My Sunday school class of fifth- and sixth-graders
was studying the Last Supper and Christ's betrayal.
I wanted them to think about the disciple Judas
and what his motives might have been. I wanted
them to look more closely at what had happened
those last few days of Christ's life. Maybe a bit of
role playing would help.

"Here's the assignment," I said. "Each of you
should imagine you're Judas. You're standing
before God in heaven after the Crucifixion. What
can you say for yourself? How can you justify the
terrible thing you've done?"

"Who's going to play God?" one student asked.

"Me," I said, "at least for this exercise."

They came up with some interesting and
rather sophisticated arguments.

The Crucifixion wasn't really Judas's fault, said one boy. Judas only betrayed Christ at Jesus's urging, claimed another. After all, it was Jesus Who said, "Do what you must do." One girl went so far as to say that if Judas hadn't done what he'd done, there might not have been a Resurrection at all.

Still, none of the arguments moved me. Then one of the youngest boys in the class looked up a little sheepishly at me. "I'm really sorry," he said.

"What for?" I asked.

"That's what Judas should say. 'I'm really sorry. I had no idea what I was doing. Please forgive me. I would never have done it if I'd really understood Who He was.'"

I'm not God. I don't know how His conversation with Judas went. But as a Sunday school teacher I learned a lot that day. Arguments are compelling, but nothing is quite as powerful as asking for forgiveness.

I am sorry, Lord, and I repent for all the wrongs I've committed. —Rick Hamlin

Digging Deeper: *Psalms 32:5, 103:10–14; 1 John 1:9*

THE SIXTEENTH DAY: *SATURDAY*

SURRENDER

But he was pierced for our transgressions, he was crushed for our iniquities; the punishment that brought us peace was on him. —Isaiah 53:5 *(NIV)*

One Saturday morning, my husband, Whitney, breezed into the kitchen, holding out a hymnal. "I forget how this song goes, and in an hour I'm supposed to lead it at the men's Bible study. Will you sing it with me?" he asked, looking at his watch.

I frowned. *I'd rather eat that hymnal than sing right now* is what I wanted to say. Last night I'd relived a wrong done to me a few years earlier. I'd stumbled out of bed dragging resentment like a ball-and-chain. But Whitney didn't seem to notice my pain. And of all the songs . . .

"Please, if you just get me started I know I'll remember the tune," Whitney said.

"Okay," I mumbled. He sat next to me, and I led in a cracked, unhappy voice.

*Beneath the cross of Jesus I fain would take my
stand,*
*The shadow of a mighty Rock within a weary
land. . . .*

The powerful old hymn pulled at my resentment. I pulled back. *But I was wronged.*

"I got it," Whitney said, launching into the last verse:

Upon that cross of Jesus mine eyes at times can see
*The very dying form of One Who suffered
there for me. . . .*

Those words I'd sung all my life drew across my resentment the picture of Jesus hanging on the Cross, looking at me with redeeming love. I began to cry.

"Is something wrong?" Whitney asked, closing the hymnal. My tears turned to laughter. In his obtuseness, my wonderful husband had inadvertently led me to the one place of peace. Surrender at the foot of the Cross. I bowed my head and prayed:

Lord Jesus Christ, Lamb of God, have mercy on me.
—Shari Smyth

Digging Deeper: *Luke 6:36; Hebrews 4:16; James 2:13*

THE SEVENTEENTH DAY: *MONDAY*

LIFE AFTER LIFE

"He is not the God of the dead, but of the living,
for to him all are alive." —Luke 20:38 (NIV)

It was another one of the challenges hurled at Jesus during His last trip to Jerusalem, this one from members of a sect that taught that the grave was final: what happens when we die? Listening to Jesus's answer, I remembered my friend Marge, grieving the loss of a stillborn son. It was her two-year-old son Andrew, though, that she'd worried about.

Andrew had looked forward as much as his parents to the birth of the baby they'd named Aidan, even placing a favorite terrycloth dog in the waiting crib. "He was so excited about having a brother—talked all the time about what he and Aidan would do together."

When told that his brother had gone to live in Heaven, Andrew showed no reaction. "We didn't

40 DEVOTIONS FOR LENT   35

know whether he was bottling up his feelings or whether the shock had simply numbed him." As days passed, Marge worried that this emotional distance might become permanent. Hoping to rouse some response from him, she bought Andrew the big red balloon he'd been begging for.

"We'd barely left the store when it got away from him." Ordinarily he would have bawled, Marge told me. She would have been glad even for that, happy for any kind of reaction. "Nothing. Not a peep. He just stood staring solemnly as it sailed off into the sky, as though he couldn't feel anything anymore."

Andrew didn't say a word about the lost balloon, not until his dad got home from work that night. Then the little boy rushed to him. "Daddy," he said, "I gave Aidan a balloon!"

To God and to Andrew, I thought, *Aidan is most definitely alive.*

Lord Jesus, give me the faith of a child.
—Elizabeth Sherrill

Digging Deeper: *John 20:31; 1 Thessalonians 4:16*

THE EIGHTEENTH DAY: *TUESDAY*

FEASTING OF JESUS

*All people may take refuge in the
shadow of your wings. They feast on the
abundance of your house, and you give
them drink from the river of your delights.*
—Psalm 36:7–8 (NRSV)

My wife and I bought a ton (yes, two thousand
pounds!) of compost for our Vermont garden
last year. A backhoe slowly made its way down
our street. When it arrived at our driveway, our
neighbor slammed the gearshift into park, keeping the backhoe's engine rumbling, and called
out, "Where should I dump it?"

"That corner over there," I told him, pointing
past the end of the driveway, "next to the garden!"

It took us days to spread all of that compost.
In the late-day sunshine, when we were done, you
could actually feel the heat of the soil radiating.
Our garden was ready for planting, and in went

the rows of beans, cucumbers, beets, carrots, broccoli, and lettuces.

The words in today's reading are from Psalm 36:7–8: "All people may . . . feast on the abundance of your house, and you give them drink from the river of your delights." I love these words. What revelry that is from the psalmist to God and as a promise to us.

The soil in our garden is like my soul, waiting for God. The compost is like all of the spiritual activities I fill my life with: prayers, Bible reading, spiritual conversations with friends, helping my neighbors. Compost seasons the soil as prayer seasons the soul. And that backhoe? I imagine it is the church, particularly right now, when the services, traditions, and people who make it up all come together to deliver what I need the most.

Abundant Gardener, show me today where I may cultivate deeper soil and well-watered roots to You.
—Jon Sweeney

Digging Deeper: *Numbers 14:7–9; Isaiah 61:10–11; Jeremiah 17:7–9*

The Nineteenth Day: *Wednesday*

Honoring the Giver

*There came unto him a woman having an
alabaster box of very precious ointment, and
poured it on his head.* —Matthew 26:7 (KJV)

When our aunt Henrietta died at seventy-nine,
my sister Amanda and I cleared out her apart-
ment. To our surprise and dismay, we found a
closet filled with boxes that contained almost
every gift she'd received for at least five years.

"We gave these blue-striped towels last
Christmas," Amanda said, peeking into an oblong
box. "The ones she was using were thin and worn."

I spotted a familiar-looking gift bag. Sure
enough, it contained the lavender-scented lotion
I'd found at a specialty shop—unopened and
unused, although Aunt Henrietta had written
a gracious thank-you. So it was with box after
box. Rose-bordered tea towels, exquisite writing
paper, carved picture frames—lovingly selected

gifts were saved, apparently for a special time that never came.

How sad! I thought. Poor Aunt Henrietta never benefited from gifts that would have made her life more comfortable. Even worse, she missed out on the joy of remembering the giver every time she used the gift.

Then I thought of someone on the way to becoming as "poor" as my aunt: me. Didn't I insist that my family use the old towels and save the new ones for company? Hadn't I often set the table with chipped dishes while two "company sets" languished in the cabinet?

My basic nature is still a lot like Aunt Henrietta's. But I learned something important from her overflowing closet: The best way to honor the giver is to make full and joyful use of the gift. And it's the same whether the gift is a matchstick cross lovingly glued together by a nine-year-old or the wondrous gift of salvation given by Jesus.

Lord, You received the gift of precious ointment with love, and You gave Your life with love. Help me to honor all Your gifts. Amen. —Penney Schwab

Digging Deeper: *2 Corinthians 9:7; Hebrews 13:16; James 1:17*

....

THE TWENTIETH DAY: *THURSDAY*

THE GREEKS

> *Now there were some Greeks among those who were going up to worship at the feast; these then came to Philip, who was from Bethsaida of Galilee, and began to ask him, saying, "Sir, we wish to see Jesus." —John 12:20–21 (NAS)*

The feast of the Passover was the biggest event in the Jewish calendar of Jesus's day. Even non-Jewish "God Fearers" who followed the teachings of Moses traveled to Jerusalem for the celebrations. So these Greeks, in town for a holiday, have heard rumors about the Messiah and come to see for themselves. The ministry executives (Philip and Andrew) huddle to consider the request and take the usual executive action: They bump it up the organizational chart to the Master. Jesus's response is almost a series of riddles: seeds dying, losing your life to find it, serving by following. But, because they are truly seeking Him, He promises them, "My Father will honor the one who serves me" (John 12:26, NIV).

Years ago, I visited a famous church in Scotland where John Wesley and Charles Spurgeon had preached. I climbed into the pulpit so that I could look out and imagine speaking, like those towering figures, to a full and attentive congregation held spellbound by my oratory. Then my eye was caught by a small brass plate set into the pulpit desk. On it were these words: "Sir, we wish to see Jesus." More than two thousand years after these Greeks made their first request to the disciples, people are still looking for the same thing from those claiming to have something to say about faith.

Lord, let my life show You to someone today.
—Eric Fellman

Digging Deeper: *Romans 1:16, 10:13*

THE TWENTY-FIRST DAY: *FRIDAY*

SIGNS OF HOPE

> *Trust in him at all times; ye people, pour out*
> *your heart before him. —Psalm 62:8 (KJV)*

"I saw a robin!" My mother's voice on the phone had the singsong quality of smug victory. She might as well have added, "Na-na-na-na-na!" She likes to win this game.

Mom and I have an annual competition to see who can spot the year's first robin. It started the year I left home, and it's been going on for more than two decades. Here in Connecticut, the first robin is a big deal. It means that the winter will, indeed, end, even when we're convinced it's going to go on forever. Mom and I are not winter lovers by any stretch of the imagination. For both of us, it's always been a long, gray crawl from Christmas to Easter. So the first robin is an important signpost, and even more so this year.

My grandmother has been ill for months, and my mother's older sister died shortly after Christmas. Our lives have been touched by melancholy, and the road ahead looks bumpy and gray as mortality looms large in our lives. To make matters worse, it's also been the coldest winter in a decade. It's hard even to imagine Easter. Then Mom's call came. I couldn't remember the last time she sounded so excited.

This year's sighting was the earliest yet. Three days later, I saw a dozen robins gathered together in some undergrowth by the road. A dozen! It was nine degrees out. Mom may have had the victory, but we both won this year.

God's lesser creatures know what we advanced folk sometimes forget: Easter and spring always come. Sometimes, we just have to wait awhile.

Lord Jesus, let me never forget that You are risen and present in all circumstances and in all seasons.
—Marci Alborghetti

Digging Deeper: *Genesis 8:22; Isaiah 55:10—11; Daniel 2:21*

THE TWENTY-SECOND DAY: *SATURDAY*

GIVING EVERYTHING

"She out of her poverty has put in everything she had."
—Mark 12:44 *(RSV)*

When they entered Jerusalem, Jesus and His disciples went immediately to the Temple. The disciples were overcome with the grandeur of the imposing structure. King Herod had withheld no expense in the design and construction of this architectural wonder.

Lost in amazement, the disciples followed Jesus through the teeming crowds until they came to the large trumpet-shaped coffers where offerings were given to support the Temple. Standing in the shadows, Jesus watched as wealthy Passover pilgrims from all over the Mediterranean world deposited gold and silver coins into the Temple treasury.

Suddenly, an impoverished woman pushed her way to the front and let two tiny coins fall from her fingers. Looking into her eyes, Jesus sensed that these copper *lepta* were all that the woman possessed. Her life savings were less than a day's wage, and she gave it all to God.

Moved by her action, Jesus turned to His disciples and said, "Truly I say to you, this poor widow put in more than all the contributors to the treasury; for they all put in out of their surplus, but she, out of her poverty, put in all she owned, all she had to live on" (Mark 12:43–44, NAS).

Much of what I have given to God has been what I can afford to give, what is left over at the end of the day, the tenth that I have budgeted as my tithe. Seldom have I given as this widow, knowing that there is nothing remaining, no savings account to back me up, no one to bail me out.

When Jesus looked into the widow's eyes, He knew He must give His all. And it would cost more than two copper coins. It would cost Him His life.

Dear Father, may I follow You without fear of cost or consequence. —Scott Walker

Digging Deeper: *Luke 21:1–4; Romans 12:1*

A TRUE CROWN

> *And being in an agony he prayed more*
> *earnestly: and his sweat was as it were great*
> *drops of blood falling down to the ground.*
> —Luke 22:44 (KJV)

As soon as the opposing player's hockey stick accidently nicked my noggin, I knew I was headed to the emergency room. The angle of the blow had opened a nifty gash above my forehead.

It was not a good time to be in an ER. Finally, a frazzled doctor saw me. She apologized that I had to wait. While she worked her needle, she gave a short recap of her difficult night: a fireman who had fallen answering a call, a fight between brothers, a diabetic dad in a losing battle with his blood sugar. Suddenly, she stopped. "I forgot to give you a topical anesthetic," she said.

This was true. From the moment she inserted the needle, I realized that a little lidocaine would've been welcome. I almost said something, but two things stopped me: warped machismo and some serious introspection. I'd received a venial cut from playing a sport I love, not from fighting a fire or fighting my brother. I wasn't forced to think about a pancreas transplant in the hope of seeing my children grow up. "No problem," I said. "Keep sewing." I didn't want to delay her anymore.

When I left, I caught my reflection in the paper-towel dispenser. The blood had marched across my hairline, paralleling the new set of railroad track sutures. From that angle it looked like a crown of thorns . . . but it wasn't, of course. That kind of crown is carried by Someone Who has the weight of the world on His shoulders.

Lord, my contribution to humanity that night was freeing up the time of the genuine saints among us. It was trivial, really—a small thing. But I know even the small things are sacred to You. —Mark Collins

Digging Deeper: *Matthew 27:11–31*

THE TWENTY-FOURTH DAY: *TUESDAY*

A NEW PERSPECTIVE

*Now your attitudes and thoughts must all be
constantly changing for the better.*
—Ephesians 4:23 (TLB)

I have a notorious sweet tooth. Not only do I
enjoy sampling desserts; I also enjoy baking
them and experimenting with recipes. So it's
no small sacrifice for me to give up sweets
for Lent.

This past Lent I had lunch with a friend, and
when it came time to order dessert, she asked me
what looked good.

"Everything," I told her and then explained
that because it was Lent I was abstaining. "Giving
up something goes way back to my childhood.
Don't you?"

"I used to," she explained, "but I've had a
change of heart."

That intrigued me. "How do you mean?"

"Well," she said, "I decided that instead of giving up something, I would do something."

This was sounding better by the moment. "Give me an example," I said.

"I send a shut-in a card or make an overdue phone call to a friend or relative."

"That's great."

"At first it seems like a task, but I come away feeling better about life. I don't think it's a bad thing to give up something for Lent, but I've discovered that the things I do become habits and that makes a positive change in my life."

I'm looking to make positive changes in my life too. I'll continue to abstain from desserts during Lent because it's good for me and I appreciate them more at Easter, but from now on, I'm going to do something too.

Lord, open my eyes to the needs of others and show me how I can make a difference during Lent and all year round.
—Debbie Macomber

Digging Deeper: *Colossians 3:12; James 1:22–27*

THE TWENTY-FIFTH DAY: *WEDNESDAY*

TRUE FORGIVENESS

"If you hold anything against anyone, forgive
them, so that your Father in heaven may
forgive you your sins." —Mark 11:25 (NIV)

Knowing that His death was near, Jesus spent the
precious days teaching the crowds that followed
Him. Especially important, He stressed, was
learning to forgive.

For me, Jesus's words brought back a long-ago
phone call. At eighty-two and in poor health, my
mother-in-law was calling from Louisville, Kentucky,
"to set right anything wrong between us." Because
she was the best-organized person I've ever known,
I realized that she was preparing for death with her
usual efficiency. There'd been times, she went on,
when she'd been impatient, judgmental, unkind.

"I'm asking you now, Tib, to forgive me."

And I, touched by this gesture from a proud
and accomplished woman, blurted out, "Why,

there's nothing to forgive! You've been the best mother-in-law in the world!"

For the most part, this was true: She'd been generous, caring, supportive. Inevitably, over the course of thirty years, there'd been friction between her disciplined lifestyle and my less-so one. Some episodes still rankled, like the time a traffic jam made us half an hour late for dinner at her home. We arrived to find the others eating.

Embarrassed to admit I remembered anything so petty, I assured her again that all was well between us. Mother Sherrill's request was made with seriousness and integrity. And I took the easy, self-protective, socially graceful way out: There's nothing to forgive.

But there is, of course, in any long-term human relationship. To forgive, I understood too late for what could have been the closest moment ever for the two of us, means being truthful about the damage so that the forgiveness, too, will be true.

Lord Jesus, You revealed the seriousness of sin by going to the Cross. Help me in the hard work of forgiveness.
—Elizabeth Sherrill

Digging Deeper: *Proverbs 10:12; Matthew 18:21–22; Ephesians 4:32*

....

THE TWENTY-SIXTH DAY: *THURSDAY*

THE GIFT OF NEW LIFE

> *Why art thou cast down, O my soul? and why art thou disquieted in me?* —Psalm 42:5 (KJV)

I was feeling sorry for myself. Lethargic and blue, I trudged along the sidewalk. The weather had been rainy and cold for days. The spring that all New Englanders yearn for seemed perpetually out of reach, and Lent seemed to be dragging on forever. Everything was gray and tedious and miserable as I wrestled with the umbrella that had become a seemingly permanent part of my walking garb.

Suddenly a flatbed truck came careening around the corner. Just as it passed, the tractor it carried came loose and flew toward me. I somehow managed to drop my umbrella and roll onto the soft, wet grass, barely out of the path of the crashing tractor.

The truck came to a screeching halt, and the driver came running back, all apologies. I was fine, but trembling violently. No one had been hurt, and the young man couldn't reload his equipment and get out of there fast enough.

After he left, I sat in the wet grass and looked around. Everything was different. The grass was the soft, luminescent green of early spring. As I looked hard at the grass, I could see some tiny crocuses poking up. The magnolia across the street appeared to have tight, tiny buds. And the sky definitely looked ready to clear. Easter was still a couple of weeks away, but I'd already gotten a chance at a new life, and I wasn't about to waste it.

Father, help me to remember each day what a magnificent gift You've given me. —Marci Alborghetti

Digging Deeper: *Ecclesiastes 3:1; 2 Corinthians 5:17; Revelation 21:5*

THE TWENTY-SEVENTH DAY: *FRIDAY*

THE SEEKING PHARISEE

And when Jesus saw that he answered wisely,
he said to him, "You are not far from the
kingdom of God." —Mark 12:34 (RSV)

Today a group of Pharisees come to Jesus with a series of trick questions, and Jesus amazes them with His answers. But one question seems to come from the heart of a seeker. Seeing how wise Jesus is, a Pharisee asks Him, "Teacher, which is the greatest commandment in the Law?" (Matthew 22:36, NIV).

Jesus answers, "Love the Lord your God with all your heart and with all your soul and with all your mind . . . Love your neighbor as yourself" (Matthew 22:37, 39, NIV).

We will never know for sure, but I believe this man was among those who Acts 6:7 tells us "believed and obeyed" Jesus's teaching after the Resurrection.

When traveling in India recently, I met a man from a remote region closed to influence from the outside world. He had been a passionate follower of Jesus since his teens. I asked him how that could have happened.

"My father was a fisherman," he told me, "and often we would go out on the water and come back with empty nets. Then he would tell me, 'We will look elsewhere. The fish are there. We just need to find them.' When I told my father I wanted to find God, instead of telling me what tradition to follow, he gave me the same instruction: 'Keep seeking.' One day an older friend who had gone to the city gave me a copy of the Gospel of John, and when I read Jesus's statement, 'I am the way, the truth, and the life' [John 14:6, NIV], I had the answer I needed. I have been following Him ever since."

Lord, let me find You in the confusion of my life today.
—Eric Fellman

Digging Deeper: *Proverbs 8:17; Jeremiah 29:13*

THE TWENTY-EIGHTH DAY: *SATURDAY*

AMERICAN CATHEDRAL IN PARIS

For you know that when your faith is tested, your endurance has a chance to grow. —James 1:3 *(NLT)*

Pink blossoms bob on branches framing the Eiffel Tower, and yellow tulips sway along the Champ de Mars under blue skies. These delightful distractions, plus construction barriers and a few wrong turns exiting the metro, have made me late for church. Never have I been so eager to attend a service.

I dash into the American Cathedral in Paris and slide into a pew just as the procession begins. "All glory, laud, and honor" fills the sanctuary with familiar melody; clergy and readers in recognizable red and white vestments wave the palms. Even the US state flags suspended over the sanctuary make me feel at home. Suddenly, here in this church where I know no one, I experience reunion so powerful I am too over-come to sing.

Until this day, I had spent all of Lent in Turkey without any Christian fellowship. Yet God, in His infinite wisdom, had a lot to teach me in the land of my Christian ancestors, where few spoke my language and fewer still under-stood my faith practices. It was during my recent sojourn in ancient Cappadocia that one of my traveling companions suggested, "You have to leave your country to understand it." Perhaps this is true of accidental pilgrims like me who learn truths about their faith communities by living without them, at least for a while.

As Holy Week draws near, I ponder my recent time of testing. Now Jesus begins His. Thanks to my solitary Lent, I begin to understand the loneliness, the endurance, and the faith of His Passion.

Father of all, wherever I am, You are there. I can endure.
—Gail Thorell Schilling

Digging Deeper: *Psalm 37:18*

THE TWENTY-NINTH DAY: *MONDAY*

AT THE FOOT OF THE CROSS

"A woman giving birth to a child has
pain because her time has come."
—John 16:21 (NIV)

In rare moments of quiet, I gaze into my son's eyes. In them I no longer see the lucid glow of childhood. Instead there are ferocious dark clouds of anger, which part occasionally to reveal a fog of pained confusion. I feel as if I have lost my child.

We have had to curtail many extracurricular activities because John's behavior is so erratic. We still see his good friend Matthew once a week. I also take the kids to ballet class. It is a long trip—two subways and a bus—but the effort is worth it. Ballet is the one place John's eyes regain their former luster. Seeing him happy for even an hour a week helps me hold on.

Searching for more hope, I reread the Passion

in the Gospel of John. This time I'm deeply aware that the disciples did not know how things would turn out. They lived through the events of Holy Week without knowing that Easter lay in wait. If I grieve over my son, they grieved more fully over Christ. Yet surrounded by danger and consumed by fear and anxiety, they still held on.

I decide it is not an accident that Scripture tells us that the way of the Cross contains times of not knowing what will happen, times of incomprehensible pain. Jesus asked His closest friends to go through this. He is asking it of me.

Jesus, let me be patient with not knowing and not understanding. When I must wait, let it be in Your loving arms that wait for me on the Cross. —Julia Attaway

Digging Deeper: *John 16:33; 1 Corinthians 14:33*

THE THIRTIETH DAY: *TUESDAY*

THE NEW FROM THE OLD

*. . . A time to break down, and a time to
build up. —Ecclesiastes 3:3 (KJV)*

When my brother Don was a boy, he loved to
build fragile model airplanes with balsa wood and
tissue paper. One day, when family friends were
visiting from Wisconsin, the adults noticed that
their little boy, Bobby, who had gone to play in
another room, was ominously silent. Don found
the toddler quietly breaking all of the carefully
glued pieces of an airplane he had worked on
for weeks. My brother burst into tears, but the
damage was done and there was no remedy.

Don began saving his allowance. Finally, he
bought an even more elaborate airplane kit, and
within a couple of weeks he had created his best
model airplane yet.

Like Koheleth, the preacher in Ecclesiastes,
I tend to believe that everything happens for a

purpose. So my prayer question today is, "Where is the purpose in such painful incidents?"

Sometimes a run-down house has to be razed,
so a better-built home can take its place.
Remember the boy who broke your heart in
*   junior high?*
You thought you'd surely die!
Now at the other end of life you have true love,
and it's so much more
than cotton-candy words, hand-holding walks
and kisses after dances.
It's sharing common interests;
listening with the heart
and knowing you can trust each other.
Still I must speak a hard truth to you:
Most things break, my dear.
But here's the reason:
The new can come forth only when the old is out
*   of the way.*

Holy Spirit, teach me to tear down what no longer serves.
Then, with free and empty hands, I'll build a fresh new start.
—Marilyn Morgan King

Digging Deeper: *Isaiah 55:7; Ephesians 4:20–24*

....

THE THIRTY-FIRST DAY: *WEDNESDAY*

FINAL WORDS OF COMFORT

"A little while longer and the world will see Me
no more, but you will see Me. Because I live,
you will live also." —John 14:19 (NKJV)

Lord, life is just one thing after another. Dad has Alzheimer's disease. Our daughter had another miscarriage. Our old friends are getting divorced, and a church member's house burned down.

"Let not your heart be troubled."

I try not to be upset, Lord, but sometimes I just don't know what to believe.

"You believe in God, believe also in Me."

I do believe, but I also doubt like Thomas. I built my whole life on You and on the hope of heaven. What if it's just a dream? What if it's not true?

"If it were not so, I would have told you."

Everything is changing down here, God. Our country is in trouble. Friends move away. Even the church has changed so much that I don't enjoy it as I once did. Sometimes I feel so out of place, like a homeless person.

"In my Father's house are many mansions."

I would settle for a little farm. You know, a couple acres with a barn and a bungalow. Maybe a pasture with a willow-lined creek running through it. A little red pickup truck, an orchard and a pond, some chickens and a big garden . . .

"I go to prepare a place for you, and if I go, I will come again . . . that where I am, you may be also. I will not leave you orphans."

I know, but I get so confused. So many voices, giving different directions.

"I am the way, I am the truth, I am the life. No one comes to the Father except through Me" (based on John 14:1–6, 16–18, NKJV).

Thanks, Lord. I just needed to hear You say it. No one can settle me down the way You can. I will keep trusting You, even through the storms. And, Lord? Be merciful to my dad. He is such a good man, and we all love him.
—Daniel Schantz

Digging Deeper: *Isaiah 41:10; Matthew 11:28; John 16:33*

....

THE THIRTY-SECOND DAY: *THURSDAY*

IS IT I?

When Jesus had thus said, he was troubled in spirit, and testified, and said, Verily, verily, I say unto you, that one of you shall betray me. —John 13:21 *(KJV)*

Last year during Lent, our church did a tableau of the Last Supper. Twelve of us depicted the disciples, and another member portrayed Jesus. He was the only one at the table who didn't speak.

I played Philip, whose hometown was Bethsaida in Galilee. He had heard John the Baptist preaching in Bethany, and it was there that Jesus recruited him. Philip immediately recommended his good friend Nathanael, who was not, at first, excited by the idea. But he came around. Philip, you may remember, was present at the feeding of the five thousand, and he wanted to know where they would find the wherewithal to buy bread for the throng.

"Little did I know," I told the audience, "that Andrew was already bringing a lad and his lunch to Jesus." Following the miracle, Philip saw to it that the Greeks in the crowd were given an audience with Jesus.

At the conclusion of my monologue, reacting to Jesus's prediction that one of His disciples would betray Him, I asked, "Does the traitor not know that in betraying Jesus, he is also betraying God? That in conspiring against Jesus, he is conspiring against God? How can any of our number be so blind? Can it be Philip? Is it I?"

People who fall short of Christ's high calling—and that includes us all—betray Him every day. We don't need to ask, "Is it I?" We know the answer. Thank God for His forgiving grace. It allows us to begin each day with a clean slate and the peace that comes from knowing He understands.

Forgive us, dear Lord, when You we betray. Help us reflect Your love every day. —Fred Bauer

Digging Deeper: *Zechariah 11:12–13; John 13:18–30*

....

The Thirty-Third Day: *Friday*

Hope on the Sea

And there arose a great storm of wind, and the
waves beat into the ship. —Mark 4:37 *(KJV)*

A ship model on a shelf in the TV room reminds me of the trip we took last winter with Tib's brother. Donn is a former naval officer who lives on St. Croix, so he can sail year-round.

We'd had many fine Caribbean cruises aboard the *Vive Violette*, but last year, as we headed toward Virgin Gorda, a storm blew up that tossed the yacht around and whipped diesel fumes back aboard. The combination of pitching, yawing, and noxious air had everyone but Donn running to the railings.

I was hanging on to one of the supports on deck, thinking fondly of solid ground, when Donn looked down from the bridge and saw me.

"Keep your eyes on the horizon!" he shouted over the wind. To my amazement, it worked. I quieted my stomach and mastered the nausea by focusing on that distant steady point instead of the heaving seas close at hand.

The disciples, too, knew storms at sea, those sudden, boat-swamping winds that roil the Sea of Galilee. Now, as Jesus approached His final hours, a different kind of storm threatened. The disciples, He knew, would be buffeted and nearly overwhelmed by His betrayal and death. He helped them prepare for the coming storm by focusing their attention on the long-range picture, not on the terrors close by. "I am going there," He promised, "to prepare a place for you" (John 14:2, NIV).

When storms strike we, too, can keep our equilibrium by looking ahead to the final chapter in the unfolding story of Easter.

Lord, help me see beyond the present sorrow to the joy of the Resurrection. —John Sherrill

Digging Deeper: *John 14:1–4; 1 Corinthians 15:55*

THE THIRTY-FOURTH DAY:
SATURDAY BEFORE PALM SUNDAY

LOOKING TO THE LORD

For now we see through a glass, darkly; but then face
to face: now I know in part; but then shall I know
even as also I am known. —1 Corinthians 13:12 (KJV)

Our TV has PIP: "picture in a picture." In a
corner of the main screen, I can open a small
window that allows me to watch the progress of
the Red Sox at the same time I keep an eye on my
son Tom at the Talladega NASCAR race. Since
his lifelong friend Todd oversees the disbursement
of two hundred thousand seats and twenty-eight
thousand camping slots there, I'm hopeful of a
sighting of the guys in the stands, but at the same
time I've got to know how those Sox are faring.
With a tap of the remote, I can make the smaller
window the larger, and vice versa.

It's like that with me—and others I've met—
during Holy Week. Starting tomorrow, for the

next week, I'll live life in two windows. Most of the time I'll function as wife, mother, grandmother, friend, neighbor in the very present world around me, but at the same time in the "small" window of my mind, the events of Holy Week will unfold. With the tap of my remote, a quiet moment, the events in Jerusalem two thousand years ago will become the larger while my day-to-day life in the twenty-first century goes on in smaller, muted form.

Holy Week is a familiar yet new adventure each year, as if somewhere it is all happening again and I am living it, too, this time from a different angle. It's a hard week, but, oh, what lies at the end of it!

Lord, lead me through this coming week with new insights, new honesty, new hope in Your love.
—Roberta Rogers

Digging Deeper: *Isaiah 26:3; Luke 9:51*

THE THIRTY-FIFTH DAY:
MONDAY OF HOLY WEEK

THE INNER WALK

> *"I . . . enabled you to walk with heads
> held high." —Leviticus 26:13 (NIV)*

Lying still in an MRI machine, getting a brain
scan, was the last place I expected to be two
weeks before my prayer mission trip to Israel.
I'd suddenly developed extremely high blood
pressure and started taking medication. Then I
had fallen while getting out of bed, hitting my
head and landing in an emergency room with
severe vertigo.

"Keep your head completely still," the nurse
said. As the machine closed in around me, I realized praying was the only way to make it through
the next forty-five minutes and I thought, *Picture
yourself on your morning prayer walk where you
commune with God.*

During a series of loud, obnoxious noises from

the machine, I stood at my "trust spot" where I needed to cross a busy road. When the noises gave way to a quick beat, I crossed the street. As each series of noises came, I remembered details of previous times of communion with God on the quiet subdivision road. The huge oak tree where thousands of acorns littering the sidewalk reminded me of God's lavish provision. Rain gushing down the curb cleansed the pollen and debris from the road. A big landscape rock had me meditate on Christ praying on the rock in Gethsemane. As the machine made a noise like the sound of someone pulling a bow across a huge out-of-tune instrument, I felt utterly dependent on God, yet at peace with letting go of all of my own grand plans. *You'll be at that very place in Gethsemane soon.*

Finally, the machine stilled and the padded table moved out of it.

Dear Father, enable me to have a vivid inner walk with You in all of life's circumstances. Amen. —Karen Barber

Digging Deeper: *Deuteronomy 5:33; Psalm 86:11*

The Thirty-Sixth Day:
Tuesday of Holy Week

God Is in the Details

*And as they came out, they found a man of
Cyrene, Simon by name: him they compelled
to bear his cross. —Matthew 27:32 (KJV)*

Which cliché do you abide by: The devil is in
the details or God is in the details? No matter;
something extraordinary is in the details.

Take for instance that single line about Simon
of Cyrene. Maybe the Romans forced Simon to
help; maybe he would've offered this small gift
anyway. In either case, Jesus accepted. A cynic
might note that Jesus didn't have much choice,
but that misses the point: Jesus had lots of choices.
He could have wiggled out of the whole mess with
Pilate. He could have chosen a quicker execution.
He could have skipped the whole proceeding.
He did not.

Our youngest daughter, Grace, has talked

about becoming a hospice worker when she grows up. She's seen two grandparents die in hospices. She has seen the kind of people who work there: kind people. Maybe it's a job; maybe economic circumstances compelled them to work there—does it matter? Fact is, they're there, in someone's time of need, to assist others on their journey, to make their passing less difficult.

Are we compelled to help others or do we offer? I'm guessing that the person whose burden is suddenly lightened by our presence doesn't really care what brought us to that moment. Those are just details . . . and I think God is, most assuredly, in the details.

Lord, You said that what we do for the least of our brothers and sisters we do for You. Help us to see You in everything we do in our everyday lives, even in the tiniest details.
—Mark Collins

Digging Deeper: *Psalm 147:4—5; Luke 12:6—7*

The Thirty-Seventh Day:
Wednesday of Holy Week

Silence

"When you are praying, do not heap up empty phrases as the Gentiles do; for they think that they will be heard because of their many words." —Matthew 6:7 (NRSV)

Years ago, when I lived alone, I decided not to speak from Wednesday night in Holy Week to Easter Sunday morning. It wouldn't be too difficult now with e-mail and texting, but then it took a little planning. Early in the week I did my grocery shopping, made phone calls and took care of any tasks that required speech. I took Maundy Thursday off from work; Good Friday was a holiday.

I wanted to be silent because sometimes my mouth works faster than my brain, and it's only when I've finished saying something that I realize I ought to have kept it to myself. That week I wanted to take preventive measures. By keeping my mouth shut, I could be assured of not hurting or offending anyone during those holy days. It worked.

But, of course, God had a lot more to teach me. What I'd considered a sacrifice became a form of worship, and into my silence God poured a torrent of grace. I understood more deeply than ever before the meaning of Holy Week. I felt the flutter of the linen cloth when the disciple fled naked, abandoning Jesus in the Garden of Gethsemane. I saw the shadows of members of the Sanhedrin rushing through the night to their secret meeting. I felt the agony of Peter, bent over in shame at his betrayal, while the cock crowed for the third time. I shivered in the chill of the sudden darkness at the foot of the Cross. I heard the wailing of the women and Mary's soft sobs as she bent over her Son's body. Into my silence flowed the power of Jesus's sacrifice, and I wondered if I'd ever speak again.

Lord Jesus, fill me with compassion as I become Your silent witness. —Marci Alborghetti

Digging Deeper: *Psalm 141:3; Proverbs 17:27*

The Thirty-Eighth Day:
Maundy Thursday

Passionate Prayer

And being in agony, He prayed more earnestly.
—*Luke 22:44* (NKJV)

A garden seems a strange setting for Jesus's agony. Gardens are supposed to be tranquil, not echoing with cries; the ground strewn with blossoms, not splotched with blood. Jesus makes His way in the night to Gethsemane, a garden of olive trees. His steps are slow and heavy, weighted in sorrow.

I don't want to watch Jesus throw Himself to the ground, alone in His suffering. His best friends, His disciples, have fallen asleep. His voice, so resonant when He was teaching, sounds weak and hoarse. "Father, if it is Your will, take this cup away from Me" (Luke 22:42, NKJV). Torment seeps from the pores of His skin in great drops of blood. It stains His robe and drips in the dirt. All the while, Jesus never stops praying.

How fervently I prayed last spring, when an inflamed nerve caused severe pain in my leg and foot. Lying helplessly in bed, I poured all my energy and concentration into calling on God to help me to cope with the pain. One night, when the pain was particularly bad, I coped by repeating the name of Jesus over and over. Another afternoon, hobbling around the house trying to ward off a muscle spasm, I gazed at a painting of Jesus looking out over Jerusalem and imagined myself settled in the crook of His arm. In my suffering, I wanted no one but Him.

Suffering—be it physical or emotional—throws me to the ground every time, but it also pulls me into a deeper dependence on God. An angel came and strengthened Jesus in the garden when He was cast down, but it was believing, passionate prayer that got Him to His feet.

Jesus, lead me to pray passionately in the midst of anguish, knowing that in prayer I grasp the hand that pulls me up to You. —Carol Knapp

Digging Deeper: *Romans 8:26; 1 Thessalonians 5:16–18*

THE THIRTY-NINTH DAY: *GOOD FRIDAY*

HANDS

They pierced My hands and My feet.
—Psalm 22:16 (NKJV)

Even more than the suffering described by the Psalmist, the piercing of Jesus's hands is a horrible scene. It seems to fire the imagination of artists and moviemakers like no other torment Jesus endured. I think there was something unspeakably dark about the deed, even beyond the pain. Without free hands, Jesus could not rub sweat from His eyes or shoo flies from His mouth or adjust His position. He was utterly helpless.

Furthermore, to puncture those hands was to mock His whole life. After all, those hands had healed the blind and blessed children. Those hands raised the dead, animated His talks about heaven and passed along miraculous gifts.

When I was just a boy, I attended a Christian camp where the chapel speaker described the

Crucifixion in graphic detail. When he got to the part about Jesus's hands, I began to cry. I rubbed my palms and felt overwhelming gratitude for the Lord's sacrifice. Afterward, I asked my father if I could be baptized.

Hands are unique, with their amazing blend of sensitivity and strength. My mother could read one degree of fever with the back of her fingers, and she could thread a tiny needle faster than a magician. Although she complained about her tired back and tired feet, she never once mentioned tired hands.

I'm really not surprised to find that hands had something to do with our redemption. I use my hands to teach my grandson to build a birdhouse. I show my love to my wife, Sharon, by holding her hand. Hands seem to have infinite possibilities for good when I dedicate them to God.

My Lord and my God, when I think of Your hands, I know that You really do love me. I give You my hands to be used for good. —Daniel Schantz

Digging Deeper: *Luke 24:50; Romans 12:1–2*

THE FORTIETH DAY: *HOLY SATURDAY*

JESUS'S BODY IS TAKEN DOWN FROM THE CROSS

So Joseph bought some linen cloth, took down the body, wrapped it in the linen, and placed it in a tomb cut out of rock. —Mark 15:46 (NIV)

This is one of the darkest moments, the time when hope gives way to despair. The old age is finished just as surely as the temple curtain was torn in two from top to bottom in the moment Jesus died. And still there is no indication that the new age is about to break over Jerusalem.

How black that night of unkept promises must have been, and yet one man, Joseph, "a man who looked forward to the Kingdom of God," wasn't afraid to approach Pilate and ask for the body of a condemned criminal.

Just how brave is brave? I ask myself, considering the chance that Joseph took to provide Jesus a proper burial before the onset of the Sabbath.

Or was it faith? Might Joseph have already believed the as yet unbelievable?

I was only a little girl when I knew Ma Peace, but I will never forget her. She had the reputation of being a godly woman. My mother often talked of her kindness, her goodness to others, her steady faith.

And then one day, we heard terrible news: Ma Peace's daughter and her little grandchildren had all been burned to death in a house fire. I remember how my mother cried for Ma Peace, as if she would be lost as surely as her family had been lost. And yet, soon after, we paid her a visit and she was the same: a kind, good, faithful woman. And all her life she never changed: serving, loving, looking ahead.

When death is the only reality and no promises have been kept, how brave is brave? On this seventh day of Holy Week, I long for a faith that holds true even in the darkness.

Jesus, Your story is the light that overcomes the dark. Make me brave in its knowing. —Pam Kidd

Digging Deeper: *Psalm 139:12; John 1:5; Colossians 1:11—14*

HE IS RISEN INDEED!

Sing . . . his praise in the congregation.
—*Psalm 149:1 (KJV)*

Easter morning! Hundreds of tulips and hyacinths, and the open trumpets of the Easter lilies spill down the steps from the altar of St. Mark's in Mount Kisco, New York, proclaiming the gladness of renewal. The choir enters singing, "Christ is risen!"

The choir—for forty-five years I've sung with them, but following a recent throat exam I've had to resign. This is my first Easter sitting with Tib in the congregation. My once-fellow choir members process past our pew in their robes. How I would love to be with them, today of all days!

I hastily correct myself. A church choir does not perform, our director never tired of reminding us; our singing was an offering "for the glory of God." Still, it was difficult not to think of the music as somehow on display before the congregation.

Here comes the moment when I'm most going to miss being in the choir! Every year on Easter Sunday, we lead the congregation in the "Hallelujah Chorus."

Now the organ launches into Handel's glorious music. The congregation stands. And suddenly my eyes fill with tears. Not because I'm not up front in the choir loft; these are tears of surprise and gladness. Suddenly I'm filled with gratitude precisely because I'm not up there with the trained voices and leaders. For the first time I'm not following the bass line of a score. I'm experiencing the shared joy of Easter, joining in the voice of the whole people. Everyone around me in the pews is facing some sadness or stress. "Hallelujah! Hallelujah!" we sing anyway. I glance at Samuel, whose son is in the Army, and Phyllis, facing surgery, and Bailey, so long out of work. "Hallelujah!" we sing. We are people who share a great secret, people who come together today to proclaim that Christ is risen. We are people of the Resurrection, and this Easter I am part of the worldwide chorus.

Christ is risen! Hallelujah! Hallelujah! —John Sherrill

Digging Deeper: *Matthew 28:5–7*

....

He [Jesus] said to them, "Go into all the world
and preach the gospel to all creation. Whoever
believes and is baptized will be saved, but whoever
does not believe will be condemned. And these signs
will accompany those who believe: In my name
they will drive out demons; they will speak in new
tongues; they will pick up snakes with their hands;
and when they drink deadly poison, it will not hurt
them at all; they will place their hands on sick people,
and they will get well."

After the Lord Jesus had spoken to them, he was
taken up into heaven and he sat at the right hand
of God. Then the disciples went out and preached
everywhere, and the Lord worked with them and
confirmed his word by the signs that accompanied it.
—*Mark 16:15–20 (NIV)*

BIBLE TRANSLATIONS

Scripture quotations marked (KJV) are taken from the *King James Version*. Public domain.

Scripture quotations marked (NAS) are taken from the *New American Standard Bible®*. Copyright © 1960, 1962, 1963, 1968, 1971, 1972, 1973, 1975, 1977, 1995 by The Lockman Foundation. Used by permission. (www .Lockman.org).

Scripture quotations marked (NIV) are taken from the *Holy Bible, New International Version®*, NIV®. Copyright © 1973, 1978, 1984, 2011 by Biblica, Inc.® Used by permission of Zondervan. All rights reserved worldwide. www.Zondervan.com. The "NIV" and "New International Version" are trademarks registered in the United States Patent and Trademark Office by Biblica, Inc.®

Scripture quotations marked (NKJV) are taken from the *New King James Version®*. © 1982 by Thomas Nelson. Used by permission. All rights reserved.

Scripture quotations marked (NLT) are taken from the *Holy Bible, New Living Translation.* © 1996, 2004, 2007, 2013 by Tyndale House Foundation. Used by permission of Tyndale House Publishers, Inc., Carol Stream, Illinois 60188. All rights reserved.

Scripture quotations marked (NRSV) are taken from the *New Revised Standard Version Bible.* Copyright © 1989 National Council of the Churches of Christ in the United States of America. Used by permission. All rights reserved.

Especially for You

Join us for

Spring Cleaning—7 Ways to

Declutter Your Mind and Soul

Guideposts.org/Spring

DAILY
GUIDEPOSTS

A community of *friends* that accompanies

you on a path to a greater *connection*

with God, lifts your *spirits*, and reminds

you of all that is *precious* in life . . .

every day of the year.

 DailyGuideposts 🐦 DailyGuideposts

Daily Guideposts 2017

A Spirit-Lifting Devotional

Daily Guideposts 2017 centers on the theme "In God's Hands" from Isaiah 41:10 and is filled with brand-new devotions from forty-nine writers. Readers will enjoy a Scripture verse; a true first-person story told in a conversational style, which shares the ways God speaks in the ordinary events of life; and a brief prayer to help focus reader to apply the message. "Digging Deeper" provides additional Bible references that relate to the reading.

In just five minutes a day, *Daily Guideposts 2017* helps readers find the spiritual richness in their own lives and welcomes them into a remarkable family of more than one million people brought together by a desire to grow spiritually every day of the year.

Guideposts

New York

Mornings with Jesus 2017

Daily Encouragement for Your Soul

"Come to me, all you who are weary and burdened, and I will give you rest."
—Matthew 11:28 (NIV)

We hear Jesus's words and want to respond, but so often we feel we're too busy, too anxious, or too heavily burdened to take hold of His invitation. *Mornings with Jesus 2017*, an annual, 365-day devotional, is your entry into His world. Jesus will comfort you, and you'll experience the delight and challenge of knowing Him and living for Him.

In *Mornings with Jesus 2017*, you can read and reflect on one devotion each day that will encourage you to embrace Jesus's love, to lay down your worries and walk with Him, and to focus on Him as Redeemer, Friend, and Faithful One. Every day, you will enjoy a Scripture verse, a reflection on Jesus's words, and a faith step that inspires and challenges you in your daily walk of living a Christlike life.

Daily Guideposts is published by Guideposts, a
remarkable family of readers and writers who
share true stories of hope and inspiration and
home to OurPrayer ministry. You can get free
e-books and e-newsletters at Guideposts.org and
request prayers at OurPrayer.org.

Daily Guideposts

Celebrating over forty years of
spirit-lifting devotions!